DESCRIPTION

The conga drum consists of several parts. Starting from the top of the drum has been traditionally made of animal skin. Lately, more drummers are using of plastic. I tend to prefer the natural skin heads for tone and texture.

The head rests on the top *edge* of the drum, the uppermost point of the drum *shell/body*. The outside perimeter of the head wraps around a circular *wire*. The wire gives the head support to allow the rim to apply tension to the head. There are usually 5 or 6 *metal lugs* which pull on a metal *rim* that rests on the outside of the head and apply pressure to the wire that is wrapped in the head.

The shell has traditionally been made of wood, but fiberglass has also been used for the last 40 years. The shell of the drum extends down to the *base* of the drum.

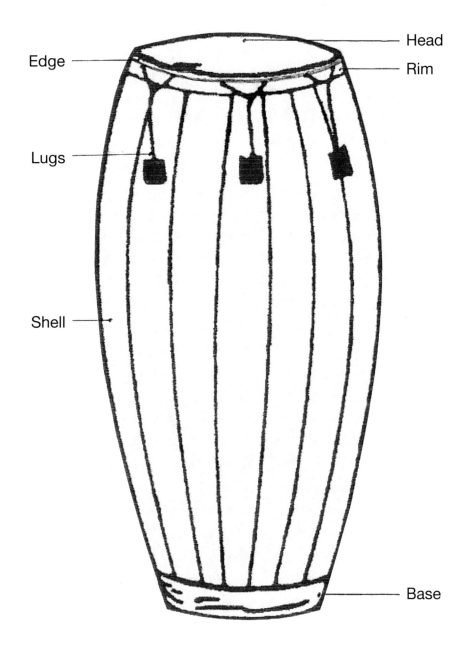

HISTORY

The conga drum (*tumbadora*) is thought to have originated from the Congo area of Africa, specifically from the Bantu and Lucumi people. Later, it developed Cuban influences. The blending of cultures occurred as a result of the horrific slave trade in the 1700s to the late 1800's where slaves were brought from Africa to Cuba, as well as other western countries.

The conga drum, with the addition of metal tuning lugs, became popular in the 1940s and 1950s. It was used in the modern Latin and Jazz orchestras of that day and gradually found its way into "mainstream" music. Some of the most influential Cuban conga players that came to North America at this time included Armando Peraza, Candido Camero, Patato Valdez, Mongo Santamaria, Chano Pozo and Francisco Aguabella.

Originally, the conga player played a single conga drum. Later, in popular Latin music, drummers began using two or more drums, each tuned to a different pitch. When two drums are used, they may be referred to as tumba or hembra (low) and quinto, conga or macho (high). When drums are played in groups of three they are often referred to as tumba (low), conga, segundo or tres dos (mid) and quinto (high). In popular Latin music one drummer will play all three, while in *rumba*, a more folkloric style, a different player will play each drum.

MUSIC NOTATION

Notes for the conga drum are usually arranged on the musical staff in order of pitch. Notes of a lower pitch (hembra/tumba) are placed lower on the staff. Notes of a higher pitch (conga/macho) are placed higher on the staff.

There are two common ways to notate conga rhythms. One method is the *Cuban* approach, which utilizes various symbol note heads to indicate the type of stroke being played. For example, an X enclosed by a circle represents the tip of the hand. The second approach, which I will call the *East Coast* style, maintains the common black dot note head for all strokes, but indicates the particular stroke by an initial above or below the note (O=open, S=slap etc.). Both methods have their advantages and disadvantages. The *Cuban* style has less text on the page, but the reader must refer to a Legend until the symbols are memorized. The *East Coast* method has more text on a page, which may appear cluttered, but is easier to learn quickly. In this book, I have chosen to use the *East Coast* approach.

POSTURE/POSITIONING

The conga drum can be played while sitting or standing (with the drum on a stand). Drummers who play multiple percussion instruments may find the standing position easier for maneuvering between instruments. The seated position is the more common way of playing the conga drums in an ensemble setting.

While seated, place the drum between your knees, allowing it to rest on the floor or slightly tilted away from you. This allows the drum to project more sound. Tilting the drum toward you can create musculoskeletal problems and hyperextension of the wrists. When using two drums, the hembra is placed level on the right side of the macho (if right handed) with the right knee between the two drums.

At the first sign of pain or discomfort stop and reevaluate your position/posture. Stretching once you have warmed up can also help prevent injuries. Keep your feet flat on the floor.

The most important aspects to drumming are posture and breathing. Try to keep your head up and away from the body as if a string were tied to the top of your head and pulling up. Try not to slouch forward. Breathe steadily and deeply from the diaphragm first and then the chest. Try to keep the whole body relaxed, especially the fingers, hands, arms and shoulders. Often hand drummers hold tension in their thumbs causing them to stick out. Allow the thumbs to rest alongside the second finger. Forearms should be placed at an approximately 45-degree angle to the front of the body.

First Lessons Conga

by Trevor Salloum

© Cover photo courtesy of Latin Percussion

1   2

Visit us on the Web at www.melbay.com — E-mail us at email@melbay.com

CONTENTS

ABOUT THE AUTHOR

Trevor Salloum is well known internationally as a music educator who specializes in Afro-Cuban and Middle Eastern drumming. He has taught drumming at universities, colleges and schools for over 30 years. He studied music at Notre Dame University, Banff School of Fine Arts and is a graduate of York University. He is a best selling author with Mel Bay Publications Inc. and has produced numerous books, CDs, DVDs and videos on drumming.

INTRODUCTION

First Lessons Conga is designed as an introduction to conga drumming for the complete novice. This book will help get you started with the fundamentals to create exciting rhythms. You will learn correct posture, hand positions, music terminology, drum strokes, exercises, basic rhythms and soloing concepts. I hope you will enjoy exploring the rich and fascinating world of conga drumming.

ACKNOWLEDGEMENTS

I would like to thank my family, friends, teachers, Armando Peraza, Changuito, Giovanni Hidalgo, Tomás Cruz, Rebeca Mauleon, John Santos, Israel "Toto" Berriel, Memo Acevedo, Michael Spiro, the staff at Mel Bay Publications, LP Music Group and Regal Tip Sticks. A special thank-you to my son, Gabriel Salloum, for assisting with the graphics and photography. Thank-you to my dear friends Tricia Dalgleish, Francisco Jaramillo and Dr. Robert Campbell for proofreading and editing the text.

WEB RESOURCES

www.trevorsalloum.com
www.melbay.com

ENDORSEMENTS

www.lpmusicgroup.com
www.regaltip.com

Email questions or comments to:
rhythmproject@gmail.com

MEL BAY PUBLICATIONS BY TREVOR SALLOUM

The Bongo Book (Book/CD) 1997 ISBN 0-7866-2071-4
Fun with Bongos (Book/CD) 1999 ISBN 978-0786661381
Bongo Drumming (Book/CD) 2000 ISBN 0-7866-4384-6
Afro-Latin Polyrhythms (Book/CD) 2001 ISBN 0-7866-5422-8
Afro-Cuban Rhythms Vol.1 (Booklet) 2004 ISBN 0-7866-7253-6
Afro-Cuban Rhythms Vol.2 (Booklet) 2004 ISBN 0-7866-7254-4
The Art of Bongo Drumming (DVD) 2006
The Art of Arabic Drumming (DVD) 2007
Afro-Cuban Percussion (Booklet/CD) 2009 ISBN 978-078667948-5
The School of Bongo (Book/CD) 2011 ISBN 978-078668273-7

STROKE LEGEND

BASS (B)

The Bass Stroke (B) is played with the palm of the hand. Starting with the flat hand raised horizontally above the drum, it then drops, striking the drumhead. There is no rebound off the head. It is usually played with the non dominant hand.

TIP (T)

The Tip (T) is more of a touch than a stroke and is played following the bass stroke with a similar striking contact to the slap. It differs from the Bass Stroke in that the tip starts with the hand at a 45 degree angle from the drumhead, while the bottom edge of the hand remains in contact with the drum. There is no rebound off the head. It is usually played with the non dominant hand.

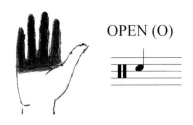

OPEN (O)

The Open Stroke (O) is played with the last four digits simultaneously. Start with the hand raised off the drumhead at a 45-90 degree angle from the drumhead. The fingers strike between the edge and the center of the drumhead. The fingers rebound off the drumhead. After hitting the drum, the heel of the hand may rest on the drum edge or remain off the head. The Open Stroke is executed with the full length of the fingers and about half the palm.

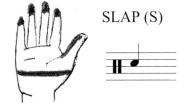

SLAP (S)

The Slap Strokes (S) are all played by striking the drum surface with the finger tips while bracing the heel of the hand on the edge of the drumhead. The slap is started in a similar manner as the Open Stroke. For the **Muted Slap** there is no rebound off the head, and the opposite hand remains flat on the drum head. For the **Closed Slap** there is also no rebound, but the opposite hand remains off the playing surface. (It can rest on the edge of the drum) **The Open Slap** is played exactly the same way as the closed slap, but the striking hand rebounds off the head.

MUFF (M)

The Muff Stroke (M) begins the same as the Open Stroke. It is executed by striking the drum surface with almost the full length of the fingers, but no palm. The striking hand does not rebound.

TUNING

Originally, congas were tuned by exposing the heads to various heat sources. Present day congas are tuned by tightening the metal lugs with a wrench. There are usually 5 or 6 lugs with a ½ inch nut on the end. Generally, you start with a ¼-½ turn around the drum, repeating this method until the desired tension is reached. First, the drum must be tuned to itself. i.e. the same amount of tension on each lug, then it can be tuned with other drums. Some drummers tune the drums to specific intervals (4th, 5th etc.) while others tune to their preference of sound. The most common tuning for 3 drums is G below Middle C for the tumba, Middle C for the Conga and the E above Middle C for the quinto.

It is also important to keep the head level with the base. If the head becomes stretched on one side it becomes difficult to realign.

The conga drum head should be loosened when it is not being played or when exposed to extreme temperatures. This is especially important for higher pitch drums because they are subject to greater tension.

STROKES

Throughout the text, we indicate the striking pattern for those who are right hand dominant. Left hand dominant players will generally reverse the striking patterns. Most notation will indicate the right hand only (R). You can assume any unlabeled notes will be played with the left hand.

In the following pages, these capital letters will indicate which stroke is played. B=bass, T= tip, S=slap, O=open. When no stroke symbol is provided you can assume this means to play an open stroke (O).

In conga drumming, we use three main slaps: 1) closed slap 2) open slap and 3) muted slap. The closed slap is played with the right hand fingertips, 2nd-5th digit, while bracing the heel of the right hand on the drum. The left hand remains off the striking surface of the drum, but its heel may rest on the rim/edge. The open slap is played with the same part of the hand as the closed slap except the fingers bounce off the head. The muted slap is the same as the closed slap, except the opposite hand remains flat on the head of the drum. All strokes can be played with either hand, but some are more commonly played with one versus the other. For example, the non-dominant hand more commonly plays the *manoteo* (bass/toe) pattern that is used in the Marchas.

Photos of Conga Strokes Part 1

Starting Position

Finished Position

Bass 1

Bass 2

Tip 1

Tip 2

Open 1

Open 2

Muted Slap 1

Muted Slap 2

Starting Position   **Finished Position**

Closed Slap 1

Closed Slap 2

Open Slap 1

Open Slap 1

Muff 1

Muff 2

Music Notation

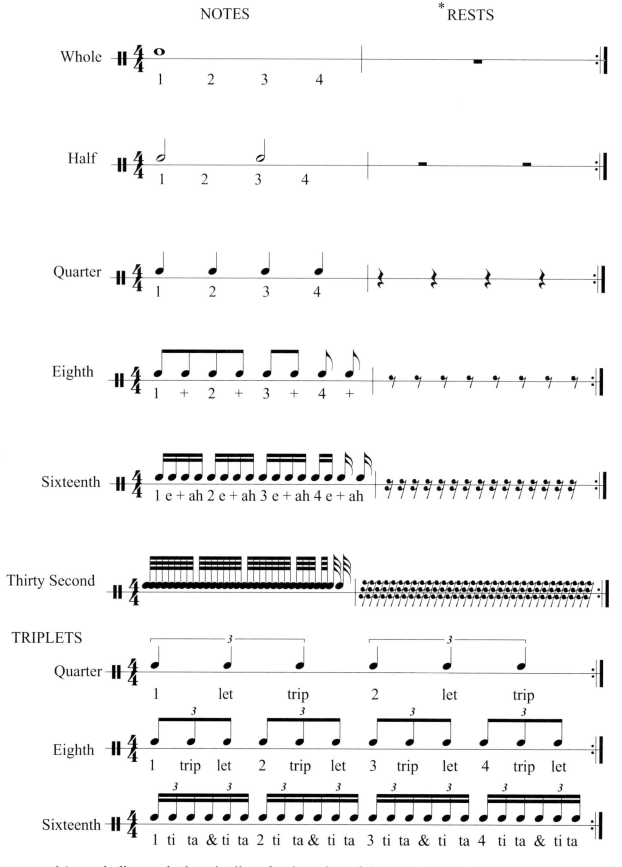

*A rest indicates the beat is silent for the value of the rest. It is still counted but not played.
 A dot after a note or rest indicates an added value of one half the rest or note which precedes it.
 When two notes are tied together the last note of the tie is interpeted as a rest.

Music Terminology

A music staff is typically composed of five lines and four spaces, each representing a different pitch/tone. In this text we will use a 1-line staff since we are using two drums. The *macho* (higher pitch) is above the line and the *hembra* (lower pitch) is below.

Vertical bar lines divide the staff into smaller subunits of music called measures or bars.

A time signature at the beginning of the staff indicates the value of each measure. In 4/4 time each measure has a value equal to four quarter notes per measure. The top number indicates "how many," while the bottom number indicates "what type of notes."

This measure would be counted "1, 2, 3, 4" in 4/4 time. It is also called *Common time* which is indicated by a large C at the beginning of the staff.

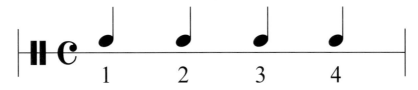

Cut time occurs in many forms of dance music and is indicated by putting a vertical line through the C. Instead of counting 1, 2, 3, 4 you would count "1 and 2 and."

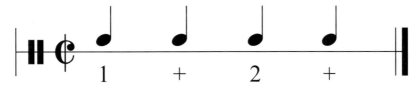

Music Terminology 2

Odd numbers of notes grouped together usually appear with a number above, indicating the number of notes in the group.

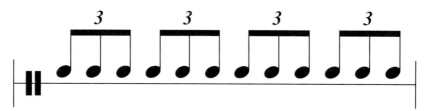

Accents are indicated by the "greater than" symbol (>). These notes are given greater than usual emphasis and are played louder.

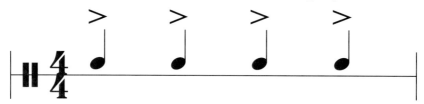

Standard repeat signs consist of two dots placed central to double bar lines. Everything within the repeat symbols is repeated one or more times.

A diagonal line dividing two dots in the center of a measure means to repeat the preceding measure.

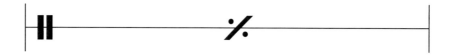

When this sign bisects a bar line it suggests repeating the two previous measures.

General Warm Ups 1

Single Stroke Roll

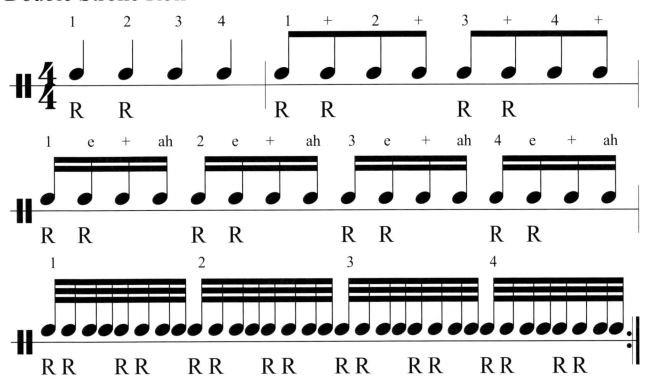

Notes that fall on the numbers 1, 2, 3, 4 are called "downbeats". Notes that fall between the downbeats 1+, 2+, 3+, 4+ are called "upbeats".

Double Stroke Roll

* Try to get into the habit of counting each pattern while you play it. When counting 32nd notes it is much easier to only count the downbeats 1, 2, 3, 4.

General Warm Ups 2

Triplets A

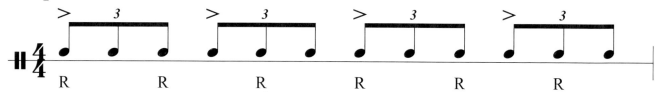

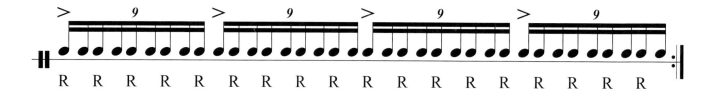

Triplets B (Double Paradiddle)

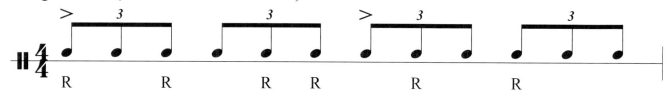

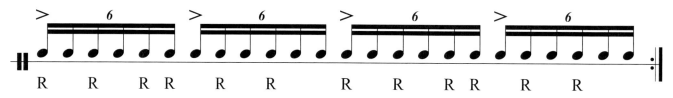

Manoteo

Play complete exercise with right hand on top line, left on bottom, then switch hands.

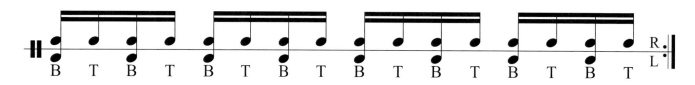

Stroke Summary *

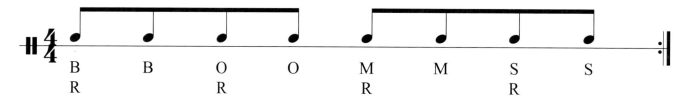

* In this exercise the slap (S) can be played as a Closed or Open Slap.

Conga Exercises 1

Play each exercise line slowly (60 bpm) with first the right hand, then the left.

Bass

Tip

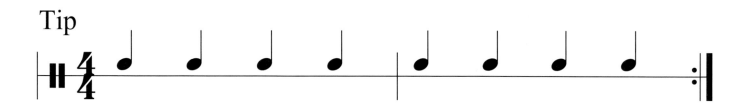

Open

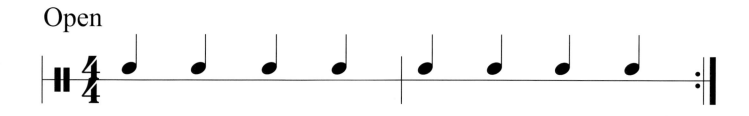

*Slap

*Try playing this exercise with all three types of slaps.

Conga Exercises 2

Play each exercise slowly (60 bpm). Alternate strokes between the right and left hand.
First play the complete exercise starting with the right and then start with the left.

Bass

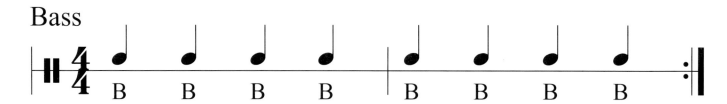

Tip

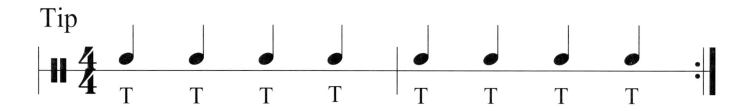

Open

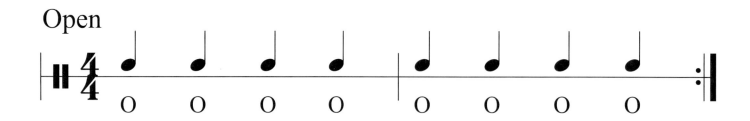

*Slap

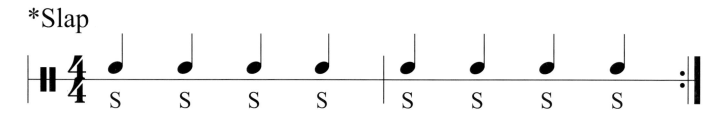

*Try playing this exercise with all three types of slaps.

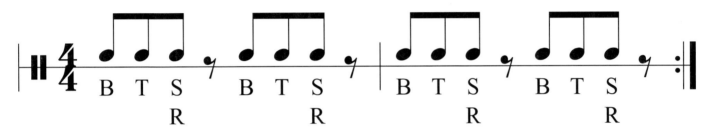

Conga Exercises 3

*Manoteo

*Play this line slowly (60 bpm) with one hand, then the other.

Manoteo with slap

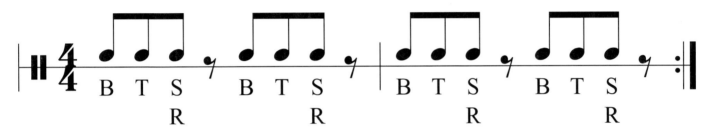

Picoteo (Masacote, Marcha Cerrada) is used in a musical piece to establish solid time without high volume. e.g. Intros or behind soloist.

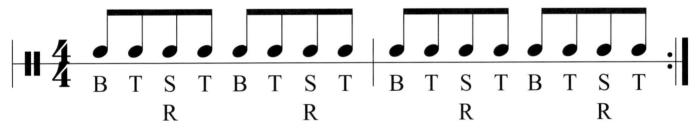

Manoteo with Opens

Track 9

Conga Exercises 4

Play each exercise slowly (60 bpm). First play as written, then switch hands.

Paradiddle

Flam

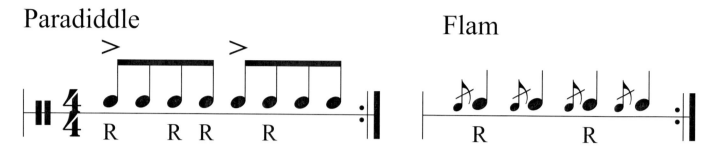

A *flam* consist of a grace note played slightly ahead of the main note. The main note is struck louder and is played with the opposite hand.

Ruff

5 Stroke Roll

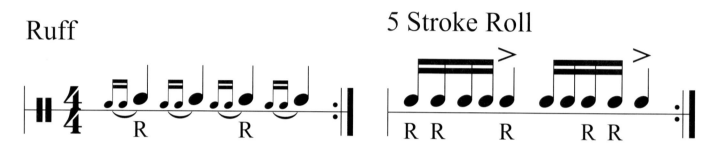

A *ruff* consists of two grace notes played slightly ahead of the main note. The main note is struck louder and played with the opposite hand.

Flam Triplet Combination

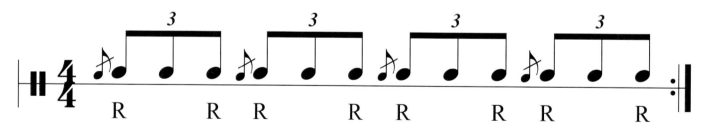

Sixteenth note triplet Manoteo

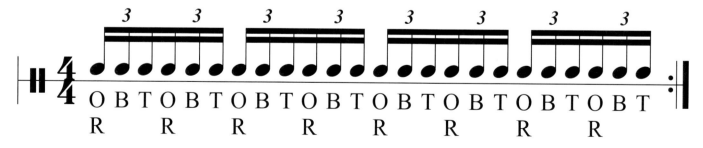

18

CLAVE

Clave (pronounced cláh-vay) is derived from the word "key" in Spanish. The clave is both an instrument and a rhythmic pattern. It is the foundation of most Afro-Cuban music. The clave consists of two hardwood sticks that are roughly 8 inches long by 1 inch in diameter. The larger one is called the *hembra* and the smaller the *macho*.

The hand position is very important in order to get the precise sound. The *hembra* is held in the non-dominant hand and propped up with the thumb on one side and the fingers along the other side of the stick. The cupping of the palm below the stick creates a hollow sound chamber. The dominant hand holds the *macho* and strikes the *hembra* in the middle of the stick to create the sound. (See photo)

There are two main clave patterns, *Son Clave* and *Rumba Clave*. *Son Clave* is the oldest and the most commonly used in popular music. It is named after the Son style of music from Eastern Cuba. *Rumba Clave* is used primarily in rumba, but may be used in some popular styles as well. (Songo, Mozambique etc.) Both patterns consist of 5 notes in a two bar phrase, usually notated in 4/4 time. The bar with 3 notes is often called the "3 side" and the bar with 2 notes is called the "2 side." In *Son Clave* the notes are played on the 1, 2+, 4 (3 side) and the 2, 3 (2 side). In *Rumba Clave* the notes are played on the 1, 2+, 4+ (3 side) and the 2, 3 (2 side). The bar with the three notes is the most syncopated (contains upbeats) and creates a sense of movement/tension. The bar with the two notes (both downbeats) creates a sense of stability/relaxation.

In Cuba, clave is typically written as a one bar phrase with sixteenth notes, instead of a two bar phrase with eighth notes.

The clave pattern is important in stating the rhythmic phrasing within the musical piece. Often the clave is determined after the song has been written. The composer will determine which way the clave fits best, but most Salsa songs are in 2/3 clave.

All instruments in the ensemble are required to be in correct alignment with the clave. Although the clave instrument may not be played, the phrasing of all the musicians, especially the percussionists, implies it. When the clave is absent, the cascara or paila ("shell") pattern may be used by a percussionist to outline the clave. The pattern is played in rumba on the gua-gua (mounted piece of bamboo) or shell of the drum and split between two hands. The pattern is typically played in popular Latin music with one hand. It can be played on the shell of the timbale, the cowbell, the block or the cymbal, while the other hand plays a supportive pattern.

Throughout the book, clave direction, 3/2 or 2/3, is indicated above the staff. If no clave direction is suggested, then either clave direction could work.

CLAVE POSITIONING

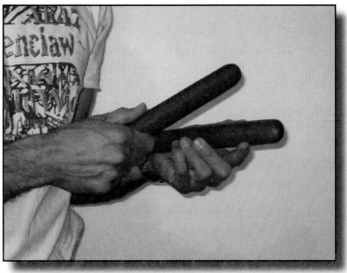

19

Son Clave

3/2 Son Clave

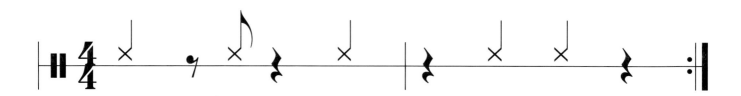

2/3 Son Clave

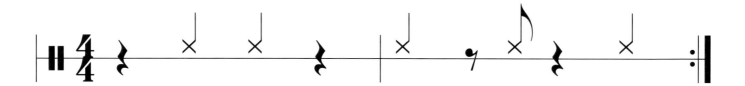

Marcha in 2/3 clave

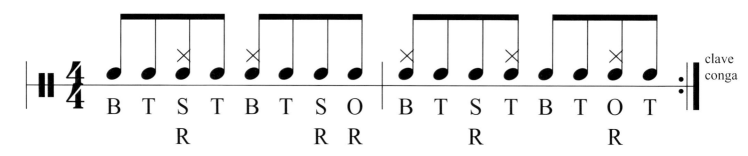

Marcha in 3/2 clave

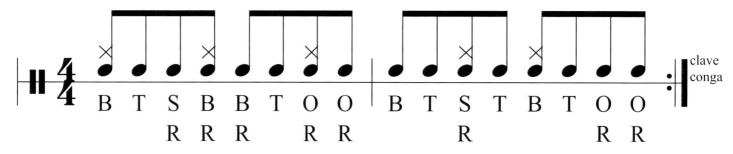

Rumba Clave

3/2 Rumba Clave

2/3 Rumba Clave

Cascara with 3/2 Son clave

Cascara with 2/3 Rumba clave

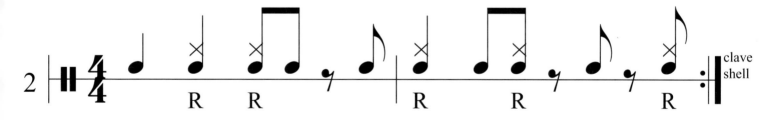

Cascara can outline either the Son or Rumba Clave. In popular Latin music, such as Salsa, it is played with one hand. (#1) Sing the simple phrase to help remember the rhythm. In Rumba, cascara is usually played with two hands on the drum shell or *Guagua*. (#2)

MARCHA

The *marcha* is a general term for a group of rhythms played on the conga drum. Usually the marcha consists of continual eighth notes to establish time. The conga player (*conguero/conguera*) is the main timekeeper of the Latin ensemble. Various marcha rhythms can be used in many styles of Latin music. Examples include, but are not limited to, the *Bolero, Son, Son Montuno, Salsa, Guajira, Guaracha, Cha-Cha-Cha* and *Mambo*. The main difference in using the marcha with these styles is the tempo. A Bolero is very slow, a Cha Cha Cha is medium tempo and a Mambo is very fast. The most common marcha used in Salsa music is called the *Tumbao*.

In a group context or when playing the *tumbao* very fast, the listener will predominantly hear the slap on the count of 2 and the open tones on 4 and 4+. The other notes in the rhythm pattern are not as prominent.

Observe your hand positions to make sure you:
1. Keep the left hand flat on the drumhead for the muted slap. This is labeled as "S" in the Marcha patterns.
2. Remove the left hand from the playing surface for making the open tone (O). It can rest on the edge of the drumhead or be lifted off the drum surface entirely.
3. Relax the thumbs of both hands so they are not tense. They should rest adjacent to the first finger.
4. Use the correct part of the palm to make the open tone (from the finger tips to middle of the palm).

SOLOING

Drummers use many different ideas when soloing or playing fills. Solos may involve only a few bars of improvisation or may extend to 8 bars or more. Fills are short phrases of improvisation that can be used for a break in the rhythm or to start or end a passage. Fills are usually not more than 1-4 bars. (See "Juan's Fill" in the Conga Exercises-4 section)

The improvisation for a fill or a solo may be simple with few open strokes and basic patterns (rudiments such as rolls, paradiddles and triplets) or complex with all strokes, more advanced rudiments, polyrhythms (multiple rhythms at the same time) and syncopation (accenting upbeats). An extended solo should tell a story by starting simply and developing a theme, building up to a climax and then a conclusion. It should demonstrate some continuity throughout, rather than be a string of separate ideas. It is very important that the soloist is aware of the clave and uses phrasing that compliments the clave direction. Listen to some of the great conga players listed in the *History* section and then create your own solos. Play along with a metronome, clave or classic recording. In time you will be making great music and above all, having fun.

Marcha 1

Basic Tumbao (Son Montuno, Guajira) 2/3 clave

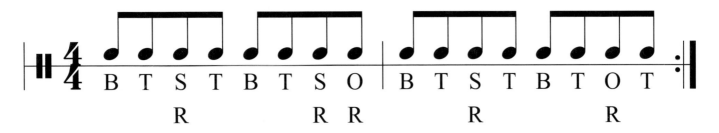

Alternate Tumbaos (Son Montuno, Guajira) 2/3 clave

1
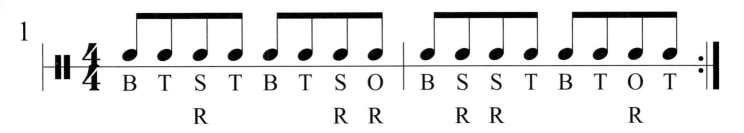

2

3
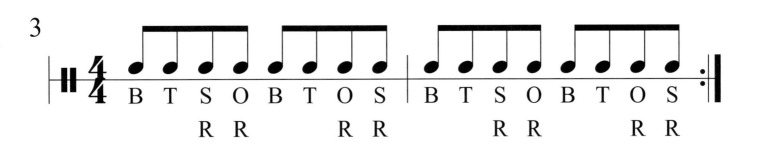

Marcha 2

Most Common Tumbao

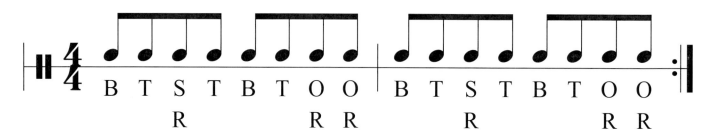

B T S T B T O O | B T S T B T O O
. . R . . . R R | . . R . . . R R

Variations

1

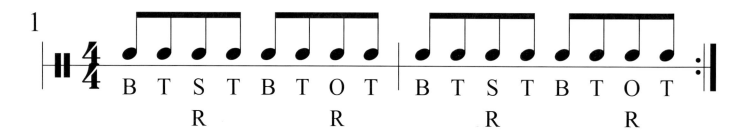

B T S T B T O T | B T S T B T O T
. . R . . . R . | . . R . . . R .

2

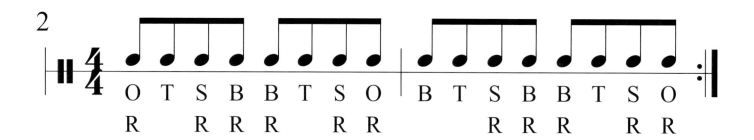

O T S B B T S O | B T S B B T S O
R R . R R . R R | . . R R R . R R

2/3 clave

3

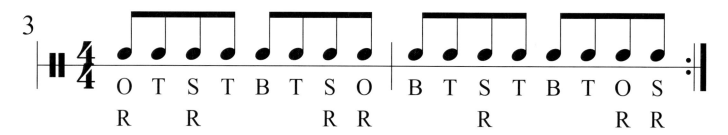

O T S T B T S O | B T S T B T O S
R R . R . . R R | . . R . . . R R

In Variation #3, when playing at a fast tempo, an Open or Closed slap may be substituted for the last slap in the pattern.

Marcha 3

Tumbao Variation

2/3 clave

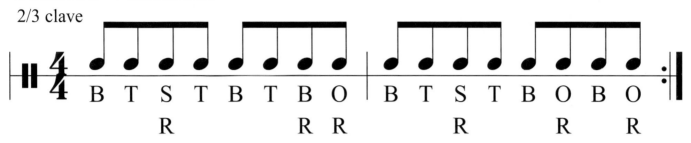

Early Tumbao

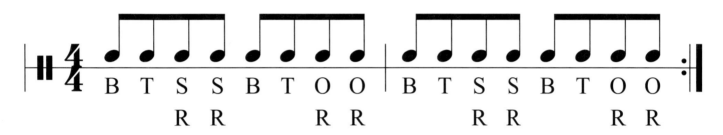

Tumbao Bolero

Marcha that mimics the two drum tumbao

3/2 clave

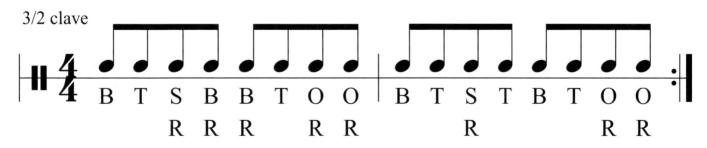

Track 15

Marcha 4

Charanga 2/3 clave

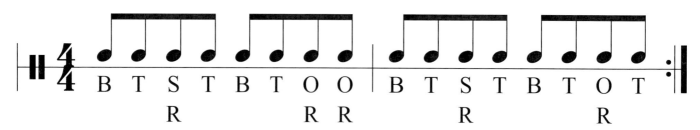

Cha cha cha

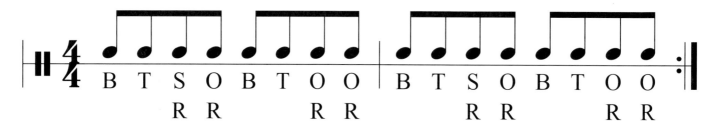

Guajira 2/3 clave

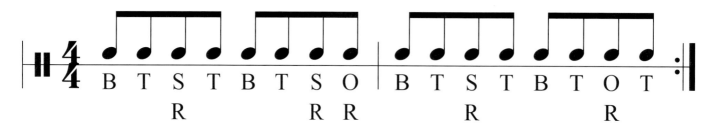

Variation for very fast tempos

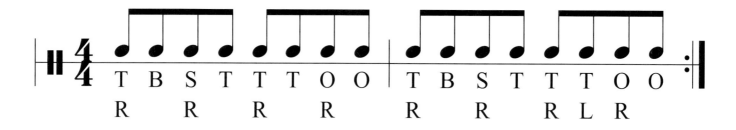

Marcha 5

In the following rhythms only the first bar changes.
The second bar remains the same.

3/2 Clave

1

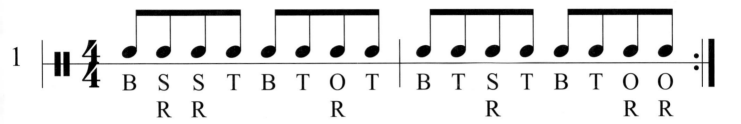

3/2 Clave

2

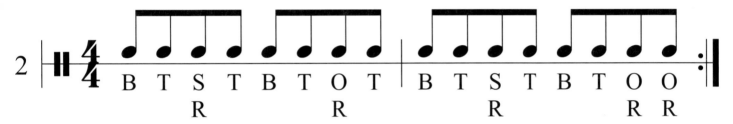

3/2 Clave

3

3/2 Clave

4

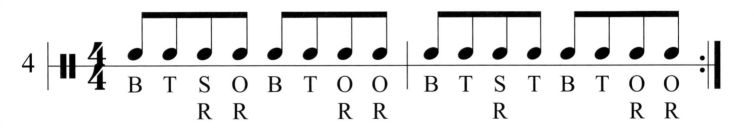

Marcha 6

Rumba Ride (Tres Dos)-used as a introduction to the Guaguanco

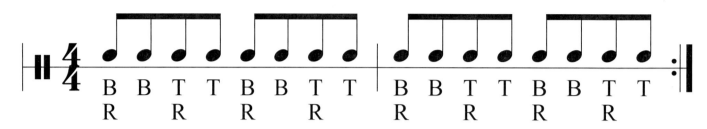

Rumba (Tumba) Guaguanco Matanzas Style

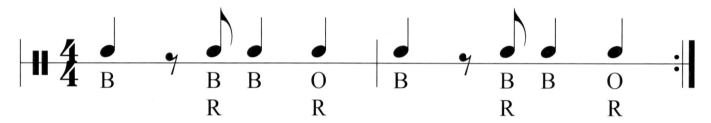

Rumba (Tres Dos) Guaguanco Matanzas Style

3/2 Rumba Clave

Rumba (Tres Dos) Guaguanco Matanza Style-Variation

3/2 Rumba Clave

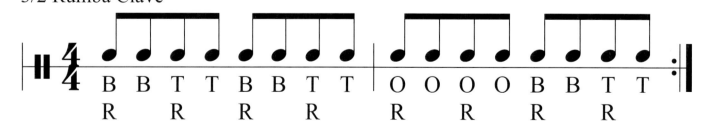

The rumba patterns presented here are just a taste of the rhythms from Matanzas, Cuba. For more rumba and other folkloric rhythms see Mel Bay Presents Afro-Cuban Rhythms Vol.1&2 by Trevor Salloum.

Marcha 7

Guaguanco Tres Dos with 3/2 Rumba clave

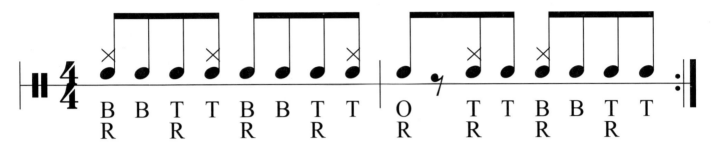

Guaguanco Tres Dos Variation with 3/2 Rumba clave

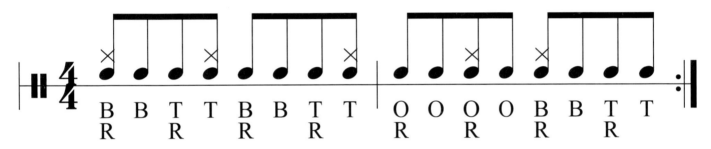

Two Drum

Basic Tumbao 2/3 clave

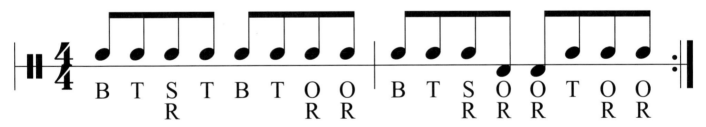

Cha Cha Cha

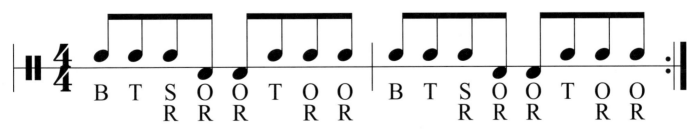

Marcha 8
Two Drum

Cha Cha Cha 2/3 clave

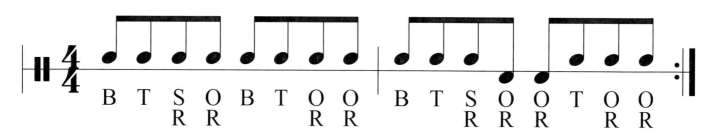

Bolero

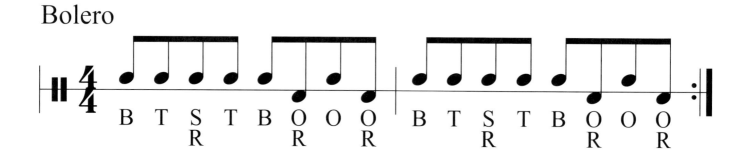

*Juan's Fill 2/3 clave

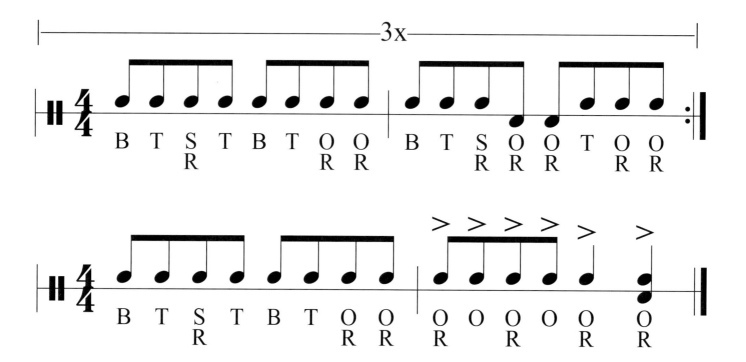

*A fun marcha and drum fill that I learned from the folkloric group *Cutumba,* in Santiago de Cuba.

Notes